Old-Age Express

Old-Age Express

Jane Durham

iUniverse, Inc.
New York   Lincoln   Shanghai

Old-Age Express

iUniverse books may be ordered through booksellers or by contacting:

iUniverse
2021 Pine Lake Road, Suite 100
Lincoln, NE 68512
www.iuniverse.com
1-800-Authors (1-800-288-4677)

Because of the dynamic nature of the Internet, any Web addresses or links contained in this book may have changed since publication and may no longer be valid.

The views expressed in this work are solely those of the author and do not necessarily reflect the views of the publisher, and the publisher hereby disclaims any responsibility for them.

ISBN: 978-0-595-46123-3 (pbk)
ISBN: 978-0-595-90422-8 (ebk)

Printed in the United States of America

Dedication

A BLESSING

Bless my children,
And my children's children,
And their children.
Help them choose wisely
The things that they do,
The places they go,
And the words that they say,
Every day.

Acknowledgments

Editorial Assistant

Jordan Flournoy

Production Team

Kyle and Kristen Hay

Consultants

Margaret Durham
David and Soni Durham
James and Janet Durham
Tom and Barb Flournoy

Introduction

ANOTHER YEAR OLDER

Observations, thoughts, and comments.
Devastation, grief, despair.
Frustration, challenge, victory,
Praise, petition, prayer.
Some thoughts are bright and sunny,
Others go from bad to worse.
But each one takes the spotlight
In eight short lines of verse.

Contents

SHORT TAKES

A LITTLE LONGER

SHORT TAKES

Above Water

The current is fast.
Strong waves overflow.
I don't dare to be caught
In the undertow.
I keep paddling frantically.
What can I say?
My head's still above water
For now, anyway.

Advice

Exercise regularly.
Walk a mile before dawn.
Never go out
Without sunscreen on.
Dig in the garden.
Then mow the lawn.
All this would be good,
If only I could.

Agility

Steer clear of all
Avoidable droop.
Conquer the threat
Of advanced shoulder stoop.
Keep hands and feet steady.
Don't fumble or drop.
Try to keep moving,
But know how to stop.

A Good Rain

Early this morning
We had a good rain.
Now the landscape
Is no longer plain.
The trees and the grass
Are a fresh-minted green.
It's about the loveliest
Rain that I've seen.

Ah-hah! Moment

I used to have
An inquiring mind.
An Ah-hah! Moment
I'd occasionally find.
Now it seems
The time has come
When my best reply
Is a mumbled "hmmm."

Air Conditioning

One way to banish
Every small peeve
Is for your air conditioning
To suddenly leave.
All other problems
Disappear in a hurry.
Nothing else now
Is worthy of worry.

Already Sprung

All right! Hop up!
Just spring from your seat!
That means exercise class
Is nearly complete.
I try to comply.
I want to feel young.
But I fear that my spring
Has already sprung.

Ambition

Way back there
I had a vision
And strength to bring
My plans to fruition.
Where did that go?
Is losing ambition
An inevitable part
Of life's transition?

Anchors

Most of the songs
Had tunes I could sing.
And telephones had
A recognizable ring.
There were balloons
On the birthday girl's door.
Lots of my anchors
Aren't here any more.

Angel Wings

When you hear the sound
Of angel wings,
You'll want to know
What your next move brings.
As you near the place
Where you belong,
Your friends will shout
"Hey! What took you so long?"

Another World

When we were young,
We dreamed big dreams.
No boundaries,
No trivial schemes.
Another world,
Another land,
Where we could do
Whatever we planned.

Apology

Your remark
Was quite unwise.
You know you should
Apologize.
Make the effort.
You won't regret it.
They may even forget
That you ever said it.

Apples

An apple for the teacher
We used to say.
And an apple a day
Keeps the doctor away.
Patriotic themes
That could make people cry
Were motherhood
And apple pie.

Aspercreme

Aspercreme
And Tylenol,
And a new look
For my hair.
This recipe
Will make today
Much easier
To bear.

Authors

No, we're not sisters.
Just neighbors and friends.
Who hope to keep writing
Until this life ends.
We each had a birthday
When October arrived.
Now Gwen's eighty-two
And I'm eighty-five.

Baby

Tiny fingers.
Tiny toes.
Wide blue eyes,
And a button nose.
Wriggling body,
Waving arms.
An almost-smiling
Bundle of charms.

Bananas

Our grocery is near.
Just two flights down.
Not in a distant
Part of town.
I'll stop by now
Though it's not my real day.
I'd run out of bananas
Before Wednesday.

Basket of Happiness

Carry a basket of happiness
When you walk into a room.
And everywhere you linger
Its scent will dispel the gloom.
When you return the basket
To its usual place on your shelf,
You'll sense the magic fragrance.
You've spilled some on yourself!

Beauty

Beauty is
In the eye
Of the beholder.
This becomes
Oh, so true
As we grow older!

Before the Storm

The skies were dark
But the air was warm.
It was the calm
Before the storm.
The sound of that wind
Still haunts me today
But all of the facts
Have drifted away.

Belonging

So what if your memory
Is not very good,
And you don't always finish
The things that you should?
What if your stories
Are a trifle too long?
You are still valued here,
For with us you belong!

Best Today's Self

Don't expect too much
Or set the bar too high.
Don't measure your happiness
By a word or a sigh.
You can't be where you were
Twenty years ago.
Be your best Today's Self,
Then let it go.

Better and Better

"Every day
In every way
I'm getting better and better,"
I was taught to say.
Now I reluctantly
Realize
It's hard to find
Where this applies.

Betwixt and Between

I know that I
Should drink a lot.
But some drinks are healthful,
And some are not.
I tend to hover
Betwixt and between
A root beer float
And a barley green.

Big Show

An impressive selection
Of well-loved tunes
Performed on instruments
From washboards to spoons.
Each PineCrest fan
Could proudly say,
"I went to KB's
Big show today."

Blackboard

I learned to spell
By writing words
On a blackboard
In my mind.
Now the things I write
On my mental computer
Get deleted
To a file I can't find.

Bountiful Breakfast

I'm preparing my bountiful breakfast
Barley and carrots and beets.
Glucosamine, chondroitin, and garlic
And all the rest of my favorite treats.
Cranberry, rutin, and prepzymes,
I won't forget to add the gingko!
Fourteen small pills plus a beverage,
And I'm out and I'm rarin' to go!

Brain on Vacation

We all require balanced schedules,
With both action and rest each day.
But for many in retirement
Work often feels like play.
I take time for some relaxation,
And catch up on the sleep I lack.
But when my brain goes on vacation,
I'm just hoping it will come back!

Brand New Life

In a beautiful land
With no stress or strife,
I soon will have
A brand new life.
When I get there,
Then I will be
In the place Jesus promised
To prepare for me.

Bumpy Flight

It can be a long
And bumpy flight
From Day of Birth
To Land of Light.
That's especially true
Since we can't know
How much farther
We'll have to go.

Busy With Today

Back to the puzzle
Just had a great hunch.
Bridge and bingo at midday.
Pool right after lunch.
Travelogue to China,
Stops in Phoenix and L.A.
I can't worry about tomorrow.
I'm too busy with today!

By Word of Mouth

When someone we know
Writes a first book,
Or records a new tape,
We take a quick look.
But if we hear of it later,
Memories that remain
Take on added value
From another's acclaim.

Celebrate Life

Don't be sad
Because he's gone.
Celebrate life!
His soul lives on!

Cell Phone

The newest gadget
For office or home
Is the wee, omnipresent,
Music-beeping cell phone.
This miniscule creature
Can also become
A computer or camera
Controlled by a thumb.

Cemetery

A whiff of lilacs,
Gentle rain,
Nothing will ever
Be the same.
A neighbor's hand,
Voices quiet and kind.
Indelible memories
Left behind.

Changes

These last years
Or months or days
I must learn to use
In the best ways.
When I awake
Before the dawn,
I feel the changes
Coming on.

Charter

It came to me
In a dream last night,
What I must do
To make things right.
Find the small brown house
By the side of a wood.
That is the place
My charter's still good.

Cheers!

Rickety-snickety
Sis-boom-bah!
I walked on the treadmill
And sat in the spa.
Nothing is hurting.
I have no regret.
I feel fit as a fiddle,
But I haven't moved yet.

Chitter-Chatter

You call me often.
I'm glad for that.
I anticipate
Our daily chat.
But are we talking
About things that matter,
Or is it only
Chitter-chatter?

Christmas Memory

There's a balsam wreath
On my door
And a lighted tree
On the living room floor.
I'm as ready for Christmas
As I can be.
I'll enjoy every minute
Of my memory.

City Girl

I was a city girl,
Then a farmer's wife.
So I learned country ways
Quite late in life.
I had just grown old
And somewhat comfortable, when
I got a computer
And my world changed again.

Clear as a Bell

Recent research
On the mixed-up brain
Suggests it is caused
By physical pain.
So if I keep my body
Strong and well,
Will my mind become
As clear as a bell?

Climate Control

You won't hear many
Of us complain
About the sun
Or wind or rain.
Our residence
Is climate-controlled.
Not ever too hot
And never too cold.

Closer to Heaven

The years go by fast.
So let it be.
What are you
Waiting for?
In 2007
You'll be closer to heaven
Than you've ever been
Before.

Compass

My compass is missing,
And my calendar's gone.
The alarm clock is here,
But it isn't turned on.
How can I measure
Both time and space
In such a confusing
Dwelling place?

Complainer

I don't want to be a complainer,
Looking troubled from morning 'til night.
But so many things now occurring
Don't seem to be going just right.
It isn't my job to repair them,
Or to tell others what they should do.
But since I'm so good at forgetting,
That's the skill that may carry me through.

Computer Whiz

My friend called me
A computer whiz.
I wonder what
She thinks that is?
To me it's clear,
No ifs or buts.
I'm a certified
Computer klutz.

Covered Dish

There'll be a covered dish supper
Thursday at six.
We're invited to bring
Our own special mix.
I remember the butterhorns
We were once noted for.
I no longer bake.
I'll buy rolls at the store.

Crossing Carolina

It was the longest
Trip I'd ever taken.
We had driven days
Through Tennessee.
Then Dad said, "Now
We're crossing Carolina."
But Carolina
Looked the same to me.

Daily Matters

Laundry, cooking, cleaning, mail
Take the same amount of time
On a small, one-person scale
Than they did when serving nine.
I can fix the little things.
The big ones I don't understand.
Daily matters will pile up
If they once get out of hand.

Daybook

Not a diary,
Nor even a journal.
But a lifeline
To the Land Eternal.
Scriptures and songs,
Daily prayers,
Words to live by.
Someone cares.

Dearest Grandson

My dearest grandson
You are moving today.
Soon you'll be living
Far, far away.
I'll never be able
To visit you there.
But I will picture you
In our Father's care.

Decisions

All around me
Decisions lurk.
I have to choose
The plan that will work.
Should I go,
Or should I stay?
Keep holding my hand, Lord,
I'm losing my way!

Despair

I'm sinking deeply
Into despair.
This is a burden
I cannot bear.
But my God is here
In this hour of need.
And if I will follow,
He will lead.

Destiny

I'm going to die,
And so are you.
And so is everyone
Else too.
We'd better live
The best we can.
No second choice,
No perfect plan.

Devastating

Disintegrating
Debilitating
Deteriorating
It's devastating.

Do No Harm

We have enough
Sorrow and pain.
All of us need
Less stress and strain.
Let me do no harm,
Speak no words to annoy.
I want to spread courage
And peace and joy.

Don't Keep It

Pass it along
To a friend who reads,
And show him the parts
You think he needs.
Or leave it where
Someone else can complete it.
But whatever you do,
Just please don't keep it.

Down the Track

I'm moving unsteadily
Down the track.
Oh, how I wish
That you'd come back.
Because you can't,
Someday I'll go
To where you are.
Someday I'll know.

Dr. Mike

(with apologies to Dr. Fell)
I do not like thee,
Dr. Mike.
My doctor, I
Should not dislike.
And so I think
I'll take a hike.
I do not like thee,
Dr. Mike.

Dream About Tomorrow

Dream about tomorrow
But focus on today.
Stop thinking how to borrow
Time from the master display.
First, plan your work.
Then, work your plan.
It's been a tried and true method
Since the world began.

Dusk

Last night it started
Getting dark
Much sooner than
I'd calculated.
The sun dropped down
Into the park.
Across the road
The forest waited.

Eating Blunder

Breakfast at seven,
Lunch at eleven,
And maybe high tea
At three.
Is it any wonder
That an eating blunder
Has added twelve pounds
To me?

Empty Screen

How easily now
Facts slip away,
Especially those
I don't use every day.
When I try to find
The words I mean,
All I can see
Is an empty screen.

Escape

I'll go into
My escape place
Where I won't see
Anyone's face.
Can't stay here.
I'm tired of trying.
Always protesting,
Not complying.

Eternity

To prepare for my journey,
I am storing away
Keepsakes and treasures
From an earlier day.
I won't need a carry-on
To take with me.
I'll be on a one-way flight
To Eternity.

Evening

Some folks I know
Say "evening"
When I think
They mean "afternoon".
Their evening starts
Right after lunch.
Mine begins
At the rise of the moon.

Evening News

Off with the TV!
Skip the anchorman's views
Of current events
On the six o'clock news.
To understand
This incredible mess
Is not essential
To my happiness.

Extra Mile

Always be there
For your neighbor.
Learn to walk
That extra mile.
Your turn will come
To borrow
An ear or shoulder
For awhile.

Faithful Friend

Help me to stand
Tall and strong
And to focus on others
All day long.
Let me feel
At this day's end
That I've been a true
And faithful friend.

Faltering Steps

Faltering steps
And a stammering brain
Need reinforcements
I cannot explain.
Mentally, physically,
Please keep me steady.
Whatever happens,
Let me be ready.

Family Grace

Thank you, dear Lord
For all this good stuff.
We'll be careful to take
Not too much, just enough.
And we give you our word
That all this day through,
We'll be nice to each other
And faithful to You.

Fast Forgetting

In a lot of ways,
I'm slowing down.
Working and reading,
And just getting around.
But in one major skill,
I've really gained speed.
When it comes to forgetting,
I'm fast indeed.

Forever Twenty

May I call your attention
To a seldom-told fact?
There's not much correlation
Between appearance and act.
Though you'll resemble a prune
And shake and stagger a-plenty,
The real you inside
Will forever feel twenty.

Four Things

Four things I have lost
And don't know how to get back.
Without them, I'm floundering,
Wavering, totally off track.
Perspective—seeing the big picture,
Initiative—plunging right in,
Priorities—knowing what comes first,
Persistence—finishing things I begin.

Friend of Mine

She's in the hospital
Someone said.
Or possibly
She could be dead.
I hope she'll be back,
Feeling fine.
I miss her so,
This friend of mine.

Fuzz Out

My friends are beginning to fuzz out.
That's not something I want to see.
But when a conversation gets sidetracked,
Surely the culprit's not me!
We're all losing a bit of our hearing,
Which allows misunderstanding at best.
So I'll try to relax and be honest
And fuzz out with all of the rest.

Get Going

I just stopped by
For a neighborly bow.
I'm fixin' to leave out
Most any time now.
I've already stayed
Longer than I should.
I'd better get going
While the going's good.

Get Together

I've lived in this town
A year or two.
Now I find
That you have too.
When can we plan
To get together?
Or maybe it's not when
But whether?

God's Help in Living

Help me remember
All day long
To choose the hard right
Against the easy wrong.
"God's Help in Living"
Is a good guide, I find.
It's kept in my wallet,
But carried in my mind.

Golden Bells

They will ring,
And my heart will sing,
As the Lord's glory
Around me swells.
Whatever my fate
I anticipate
Hearing Heaven's
Golden Bells.

Good Start

My feet look better,
My legs don't yet hurt.
The breakfast routine
Has made me alert.
These clothes seem to fit,
And they look okay.
I'm off to a very
Good start today!

Grateful Goodbye

I just got the message
That my friend has died.
She'd long known it was coming,
She'd chosen Hospice with pride.
But tears filled my eyes,
And I started to cry.
I haven't quite mastered
The grateful goodbye.

Grounded

Down the hall, 'round the corner
Five or six of us came.
And entered the elevator
At a time near the same.
We laughed and we talked
As we glanced around.
But nobody pushed the button,
So we stayed on the ground.

Guest Room

Here's the key
To Guest Room Three
It's vacant now,
As you will see.
It's been very
Nice for me
To have my guests
In Guest Room Three.

Gumdrop Cookies

Gumdrop cookies,
A popcorn ball,
Fireside games
And the doctor's call.
Waiting and wailing,
False alarms.
A newborn baby
In a mother's arms.

Half Full

There isn't a lot
In my cup
Even before
I take a sup.
There won't be enough
For another day,
But my cup is half full.
Cheers! Hurray!

Hallelujah

She died last night,
She's been taken away.
We won't be seeing her
On this earth again.
This is where
We're supposed to say,
Hallelujah!
Praise the Lord! Amen!

Hand-Held Beater

We used a hand-held beater
For eggs and such stuff.
The trick was to stop
When they'd had enough.
Omelets and scrambles,
Fluffy or flat,
And even meringues,
If it came to that!

Happy

A few days ago
My life was good.
Things were going
Just as they should.
Contented and happy,
I was almost in free.
What happened to happy?
What happened to me?

Healing

I pray for healing,
But I don't ask when.
That's decided by God
And not by men.
I firmly believe,
For what it's worth,
All are healed in Heaven,
But few on earth.

Hide and Seek

It's in a stack or a pile,
Or a very neat file,
Or in a box
On the closet shelf.
With a little more time
And a Heaven-sent sign,
I might be able
To find it myself!

High Altitude

Up on the mountain
The sun is bright.
The air is thin,
But my head is light.
Although the view is great,
I'd rather be
Back home again,
Down by the sea.

Hilltop

The people on the hilltop
Seem to live a life of ease.
Boys and girls and dogs and cats
Play anywhere they please.
Although their life seems perfect
In every way I see,
Those people on the hilltop
Are just folks like you and me.

Housekeeping

Back from lunch
I open my door
To a fresh, clean scent
And a sparkling floor.
All is in order.
The world is in tune.
My dear housekeeper
Has cleaned my room!

Hummingbird Buffet

Rushing in
Pushing through
Then fluttering away.
It's the twenty-four hour
All-you-can-eat
Hummingbird buffet.

I Am Thine

Strengthen me Lord
Where I need to be strong.
Firm up my purpose
If I'm where I belong.
Though I'm a mere mortal
And You are Divine,
Let me always remember
That I am Thine.

I Didn't Know

When did that happen?
I didn't know!
Why didn't somebody
Tell me so?
What could I have done?
Well, nothing, I guess.
Did I need to know?
Emphatically, yes!

In-Between Rats

My just-below neighbor
On the second floor
Hears scratching and scraping
In her ceiling and door.
I'm sending this message
To those In-Between Rats
"To Exit, Go Down.
Up Here, There Are Cats."

Independent

I want to stay here
Just a little longer.
I'll need some help
Until I grow stronger.
Then, when all
Is done and said,
I'll move to the place
Of the not quite dead.

Invitation

If to a party
I must go,
Should I take a gift?
I never know.
If it doesn't say,
Yea or nay,
Either way
Should be okay.

It Takes a Village

Observation,
Close attention,
Encouragement,
Too much to mention.
It takes a village
A child to raise.
That's also true
Of retirement days.

Judgment Call

About that bad
Judgment call today.
Stupidity?
Senility?
It's hard to say.

Jumping In

"Hi, Mom," said my son.
"I'm so proud of you
For jumping right in
And learning things that are new."
But that's not quite the way
My adventures begin.
I close my eyes, hold my breath,
And slowly dip one toe in.

Kitchen Band

They've started a wonderful
Kitchen Band,
With all sorts of instruments
At their command.
Though we don't know when
Their first performance will come,
At rehearsals they're having
Just tons of fun.

Kitchen Band Triumphs

As a result
Of a stellar premiere,
The KB was proclaimed
PineCrest Band of the Year!
We were so deeply touched
That we struggled to stand
In a heartfelt ovation
For our new Kitchen Band!

Knowledge

With current events
I'll have nothing to do.
Politics, fashions,
I haven't a clue.
Rich is better than poor.
Thin is better than fat.
I may not know much.
But I do know that!

Larger Life

Forgetting more,
Remembering less.
Checking each name
And street address.
Reviewing their past,
A man and his wife
On the edge
Of a larger life.

Late Date

Starry eyes,
Happy sighs,
Waiting for her date.
She doesn't know,
And I won't tell her so.
He's certain to be late.

Later Eighties

I'm entering
The later eighties
From eighty-five
To eighty-nine.
Though I'm finding
Several changes,
I choose to think
That I'm still fine.

Laundry Day

At 4:45 Thursday morning,
I eagerly spring from my bed.
And soon in the bathroom shower,
Water's splashing down over my head.
It's my laundry day at PineCrest.
Lug the clothes basket down the hall.
Take detergent, fabric softener, and spray,
And remember not to let anything fall.

Light

Make a call,
Or write a letter.
You can change
Someone's life for the better.
Light up the world
With a smile and a wave,
And you will get back
Much more light than you gave.

Little Pieces

What things must be finished
Before this day is done?
Somewhere there's a memo
That lists every one.
Old familiar projects
Are struggling to be free.
The little pieces of my life
Aren't where they used to be.

Little Words

Goodbye, goodnight,
I love you.
Unspoken
At the end.
Will you have
The chance to say
Those little words
Again?

Look Above

Use all of the time
You have to be glad.
Don't waste a second
Feeling sad.
Your world can hold
Unfailing love.
Turn to the future
And look above.

Losing Weight

When you lose weight,
Your image changes.
From head to toe,
It rearranges.
But you still need
Communication
Between Plump Prune
And Wrinkled Raisin.

Lost

I thought I bought
Two or three.
Or so it seems
In my memory.
My frantic search
Has just begun.
And I can't find
A single one.

Lost Weekend

"Did you have fun this weekend?
What did you do?"
(We're starting exercise class
With a warmup or two.)
I consider my answer.
Can't remember just then.
"Weekend? What weekend?
Is this Monday again?"

Mail Order

Vote by mail.
Don't stand in line.
To make a purchase,
QVC will be fine.
With a form and a check,
Postage stamps you can get.
Or you can just do it all
On the Internet.

Make The Connection

Snap down the lid.
Jiggle the plug.
Be sure the battery
Connection is snug.
Boot up the computer.
Jump-start the car.
Make the connection
Wherever you are.

Market

Marching through the market
Pushing grocery carts.
Headed first for produce
Then for fresh-baked pies and tarts.
Don't forget the canned goods.
Find your favorite frozen treat.
Be first in line at check-out.
Then sit down and rest your feet.

May Virus

May first I was hit
By a strange viral curse.
I safely could say
I had never felt worse.
Could there be a more
Inappropriate way
To celebrate
The merry month of May?

Mealtime Mixer

One day each month
I draw a number to see
Where my seat
For lunch will be.
I could meet a new friend,
Or two or more.
Our Mealtime Mixer
Is worth waiting for.

Medi-Bus

Dentists and doctors
Of every kind
Are in this town
But hard to find.
I don't need
To have that fuss.
I just sign up
To ride the Medi-Bus.

Midway Birthday

I won't reach a milestone
On my birthday this year.
But celebrating a mid-spot
Still deserves a big cheer.
So I'm giving myself
A gift from me.
A magnetic gold bracelet
That snaps automatically

Mission

In a book,
I found a vision
That became
My personal mission.
Although it succeeded,
It's not here today.
In just a few years,
It faded away.

Miss Nine-One-One

Good morning to you,
Miss Nine-One-One!
Aren't you glad another
Day has begun?
I'm feeling much better.
Thought you'd like to know.
Well, I'll talk to you later.
Gotta go!

Mistake

That's an unfortunate
Mistake or omission.
I want to express
Deep regret and contrition.
I know that I caused it.
Can't recall why or when.
But I give you my word,
It won't happen again!

Mix and Match

I used to be
A mix-and-match fan
With tops, trousers, and jackets
All part of the plan.
I still have those garments.
Good fabrics, well made.
But I can't ever remember
How the game is played.

Mixed-Up Nights

I am like a newborn baby
Mixing up my nights and days.
Sleeping-in through morning meetings.
Nodding-off at evening plays.
Starting the main part of work
At an hour just short of midnight.
Developing my future plans
Just a little before daylight.

Mobilized

I am organized
And energized.
Now how can I
Get mobilized?
With one deep breath,
From this chair
I'll rise,
And I'll see you guys
At exercise.

Monday Holiday

The day after Sunday
I'm beginning to doubt.
I need to stop
And figure it out.
Will we have class
And get mail today?
Or is this just a new
Monday holiday?

Mood Change

Today began with our annual flu shots,
Followed by the funeral of a dear friend.
Next came a service to honor our veterans.
All this before the morning could end.
That's a somber and serious lineup.
But afternoon will bring a change of mood.
Everyone's invited to a birthday party
With laughter and candles and food.

Morning Prayer I

Dear Lord,
Thank you for giving me
This bright new day.
Fill my heart with your love,
My mind with ambition,
And my body with strength.
In His Name I pray,
Amen.

Morning Prayer II

Thank you, Lord
For sending me
This newly-minted day.
Forgive me,
Guide me,
Strengthen me.
In Jesus' Name I pray.

Morning Prayer III

Once more I've made it
Through the night.
Thank you, Lord
For the morning light.
Strengthen my body,
Clear my mind.
Let the words I speak
Be loving and kind.

Morning Prayer IV

Keep me safe
And upright,
Responsive
And strong,
Saying only
The right things
And never
The wrong.

Morning Prayer V

Dear Lord, I may need
Extra help today.
My head feels fuzzy
And I stumble and sway.
Should I ask someone else
To come to be here with me?
If this is Your will,
Please tell me who it should be.

Morning Prayer VI

Help me,
Guide me,
And lead me
Today.
Then make me
Listen
And
Obey.

Mountains

Making mountains
Out of molehills
Is a frequent
Fault of mine.
And those mountains
Built from molehills
Aren't rewarding
Cliffs to climb.

Nearly One Hundred

He was nearly one hundred
Just months away.
He'd been a good neighbor
Throughout his long stay.
He fell in the hallway
Just steps from his door.
He went to the hospital
And won't be back any more.

Necklace

We are a necklace
With many a link.
No two identical,
As you may think.
Such different people
In thoughts, words, and deeds,
Yet stronger together,
Meeting everyone's needs.

New White Silk Rose

I got a white rose corsage
In a birthday gift set.
It is hard to fasten,
So I haven't worn it yet.
They've promised to pin it
On my funeral clothes,
So I can go Home wearing
My new white silk rose

Nighties

Well-worn nighties,
Faded and frayed.
I insist on keeping
And refuse to trade.
Soft and comfy,
They feel just right.
And I love to wear one
Every night.

Noon

The residents are gathering
At a meeting for all.
Moving slowly, deliberately,
To the big dining hall.
With backs that are painful
And feet that are sore,
Leaving walkers and scooters
In a rack near the door.

Nothing

I know that it
Would be good for me.
And it might be fun,
Eventually.
I regret I can't go,
But I must do
A lot of nothing.
Nothing old, nothing new.

Obsessive Rhyming Disorder

A lot of the time
My thoughts come in rhyme.
No season, no reason,
No prior design.
I copy these verses
In a big yellow tablet.
Obsessive? Compulsive?
Or just an odd habit?

Old-Age Express

You tried to remember
The people to thank.
Names escaped you.
Your mind went blank.
Fasten your seat belt
And hang on tight!
This Old Age Express
Is a one-way flight.

Old Curmudgeon

Someone I've known for many years
Came to visit here last week.
What happened to that jolly guy
That everybody used to seek?
He's become an old curmudgeon,
Scowling, growling through the day.
Irritating, aggravating
Everyone who comes his way.

On Your Side

We daily beseech You
To lend us Your aid
As we're searching for answers
And our decisions are made.
Help us remember
That victories and cures
Aren't when You come to our side,
But when we move to Yours.

One-Track Mind

There was something important
I was going to do.
Before being interrupted,
I was halfway through.
My attempts to remember it
All have failed.
In my one-track mind,
That thought got derailed.

Open Door

Let me love
And laugh a lot,
And learn to be
The things I'm not.
There's so much more
I could explore.
Take me through
That open door.

Ordinary Day

It's been an ordinary day,
And that feels good.
It's reassuring to have
Things go as they should.
I like some excitement,
Intrigue, suspense, strife.
But only in fiction,
Not in my life.

Organizing

You could use files,
Or little piles.
Either way
Would do.
Just put it back,
Or take it out.
Whatever
Works for you!

Paper

There's paper on the counter,
And on the table by my chair.
Little pads of paper
Pursue me everywhere.
I need to have one by me
When a thought comes to my mind.
If I can't quickly write it down,
It will be impossible to find.

Pass It Forward

Do a good deed for someone.
A kind, helpful thing
That you, and you only
Are positioned to bring.
The person you helped
Will then do the same
For two or three others.
It's the "Pass Forward" game.

Path of Life

Down the path
Of life I go,
Sometimes fast
And sometimes slow.
My God is good.
He holds my hand.
That's all I need
To understand.

Pearl Harbor

On the morning of Pearl Harbor,
Sunlight streamed across the sea.
It was the quiet winter Sunday
That would go down in infamy.
The seventh of December in 1941
Would change our lives forever
By the setting of the sun.

People Potpourri

Describing a PineCrest resident
Is a complicated task.
A definitive conclusion
Would be too much to ask.
We have a lot in common,
Yet enough diversity.
We're a unique sort of mixture,
A people potpourri.

Perfection

Try to keep
The goal in sight.
You'll do some things wrong
But more will be right.
No one is perfect,
Not even you.
So just do the best
That you're able to do.

Perfectly Clear

I made a remark
And he took it wrong.
He said, "You are singing
The same old song."
So I said to him,
"I'm taking it back.
This pot won't call
The kettle black."

Perks

There are some perks
In passing eighty.
Not too many,
Just a few.
Your grown-up kids
Will come to help you
Do the things
That you can't do.

Perspective

On the cutting edge of progress,
I led crusades to bring the best.
If I found a broken promise,
I'd get it fixed before I'd rest.
I sponsored new associations,
Hung a placard on my door.
But the things I thought were major
Aren't important any more.

Persuasion

I don't believe
Loud infomercials,
Detailed testimonials,
Or lengthy commercials.
I'd rather not know
What they think about it,
Especially when
They always shout it.

Pesky Small Poems

I'd like to write stories
Of the serious kind
To champion causes
That are on my mind.
But these pesky small poems
Will not go away.
They pop up on my tablet
Every day.

Petition

An instant reply
I hope to get,
Although that hasn't
Happened yet.
I know I'm expected
To do my part.
That's on my mind
And in my heart.

Plucky Pink Petunias

Plucky pink petunias,
Hang in there
Through
The storm.
The pounding rain
And hail will chill,
But the sunshine
Will be warm.

Post-Teen Rebellion

I'm rejecting commitments.
Sidelining my tasks.
Declining to do
Something new when I'm asked.
I never imagined
This day would arrive.
I'm in a post-teen rebellion
At age eighty-five.

Prayer

I take my problems
To God in prayer.
I know He hears me.
I know He is there.
His answers come
When I'm patient and still.
He shows me the way
And He always will.

Precision

I find it essential
To dot every "i".
As well as
To cross every "t".
But to think I might get
All my ducks in a row
Is a very slim
Possibility.

Procrastination

I should do that now,
But it can wait.
It's easy for me
To procrastinate.
It would make sense
To put this rule in play.
Don't put it off 'til tomorrow
If you can do it today.

Programs

Presenting a program in a retirement home
Is like entertaining at a school.
Levels of interest vary.
Short attention spans are the rule.
If you dare to ramble overtime,
You'd better not be a bore!
Some will wriggle, stretch, and yawn,
And make a beeline for the door.

Proofreading

I take great pains
With each detail.
I carefully proofread
Without fail.
The big mistake
That I really hate
Involves a name
Or place or date.

Propriety

When you are widowed
You should wait
One whole year
Before you date.
Or maybe not,
If you're eighty-eight.

Publishing

I've already wandered too deep in the woods.
I'll never finish this project alone.
I'm looking to find help somewhere,
On the internet or maybe the phone.
There's no time to delay, pause, or ponder,
I need to get this new book on the shelf.
Please send me your recommendations,
I can't handle this all by myself.

Put it Away

It's not where to put it.
Many choices of place
Are right here within
My small living space.
The problem I have
Is not where, but when.
When will I ever
Find it again?

Puzzlers

Colleen and Gayla
And Nancy G.
Are a talented
Puzzle team.
Using concentration
And cooperation
To create a masterpiece
From a dream.

Quarrel

I stopped to rest, with hours to go.
Now I can't get re-started.
Was it a hundred years ago
That you and I first parted?
We had a major disagreement.
You refused to see it my way.
You went in and slammed the door.
And I sped off to hit the highway.

Radio and TV

We all gathered at night by the radio
To hear "One Man's Family" each week.
"Vic 'n Sade," "Amos 'n Andy," "Jack Benny"
Were others we'd eagerly seek.
When TV came, we met Jackie Gleason,
Then Archie Bunker and Edith, his spouse.
But could we have ever imagined
"Desperate Housewives,"
"Brothers and Sisters," and "House"?

Rain Dance

We're standing around
Waiting for rain.
It is desperately needed
By forest and plain.
The weather man says,
"Less than ten percent chance".
If our ancestors were here,
They'd do a rain dance.

Reactionary

Brand new exercises
That I can't do.
Different activities
Replace the ones we knew.
Exotic vegetables
In a stir-fry mix.
My response is negative.
Old dog, new tricks.

Reading

Once I wanted to read
Every paper and book
Within my reach
(Or at least take a look).
But this need to read
Has drastically declined
Due to dimming sight
And undependable mind.

Reality

A science researcher
Is asking
Do human eyes
Perceive reality?
Do you think that we see
What really is there,
Or just the part
That we want to see?

Reassurance

It was just a little
Bump in the road.
No need for concern
Or change of abode.
By a casual appraisal,
By the rule of thumb,
I'm all right now.
You don't need to come.

Receptacle

Our trash disposal
Is called a receptacle.
At least that's
The name on the door
Of the place
Where we neatly
Deposit our sacks,
Newspapers, boxes and more.

Regular Place

I try to find dining room seating
At a different table each day
In order to meet lots of people
And to hear what they each have to say.
But at times when the dining room's crowded
And I fear I won't find any space,
I suddenly find myself wishing
That I could go to a regular place.

Rejuvenation Station

Shampoo, cut, and curl.
Hear late-breaking news.
Then take a refreshing
Dryer-chair snooze.
Get a new manicure
And up-to-date information
Each time you visit
Rejuvenation Station.

Relative Difference

Though we don't share opinions
On cultural trends
And political candidates,
We have mutual friends.
From far left to far right,
The swift compass swings.
We love the same people,
But not the same things.

Remember?

Remember those people
That we used to know?
Their kids played with our kids.
O'Reilly? O'Malley? It started with "O".
Remember the first time
Our dog chased their cat?
A neighborhood feud
Might have started with that!

Remodeled Brain

We go to the hospital
For replacement parts.
Eyes and knees
And hips and hearts.
I wonder when
We can obtain
A new and improved
Remodeled brain.

Reorganize

All my black pants
Are in here somewhere.
Where did they go?
They should be right there.
I may decide
To reorganize.
Not by color,
But by size.

Residual Part

I'm losing my hearing
And my eyesight as well.
Plus some of my brain cells,
As you can probably tell.
The rest of my being,
The residual part,
Is lungs and kidneys,
And stomach and heart.

Resolutions

On my trousers
Not to trip.
On slippery floors
Not to slip.
On my clothing
Not to spill.
In my neighbor's ears
Not to shrill.

Responsibility

I want to retire
From every activity
That requires of me
Responsibility.
But till replacements volunteer,
If it's going to be,
I'll need to keep working.
It's still up to me.

Restoring My Soul

Removing
The dread of misgivings.
Reducing
The threshold of fear.
Relieving
The tension of worry.
Reminding
That Jesus is here.

Reveille

Gotta get up
Gotta get up
Gotta get up
This morning!
This is the day
Something new and good
May arrive
Without warning!

Robin's-Egg Blue

That's a great color!
It looks nice on you.
We used to call it
Robin's-egg blue.
I had a dress
Of crêpe de Chine.
And the biggest hair-bow
You've ever seen!

Rock

You are the rock
Of your family.
Maybe you
Have always been.
Every family
Needs to have one.
It's the mission
You've been given.

Rose-Colored Glasses

Do not fret
About tomorrow.
Don't regret
Yesterday.
Put on your
Rose-colored glasses,
And be thankful
For today.

Roses and Buttercups

Roses and buttercups,
A long, white veil.
Strains of Lohengrin,
Undeliverable mail.
Tears and heartaches,
A long steep trail.
Roses and buttercups,
And a house for sale.

Sandbox

Three little children
In a sandbox at play.
What were they thinking?
What did they say?
The photo is fading
More every year.
Traces of memories
Will soon disappear.

Sands of Google

To be known
As a celebrity
Will never be
A goal of mine.
But to leave
A footprint on
The sands of Google
Would be fine.

Scene

Try to be patient,
You're almost there.
Clinch your fists,
Hang onto your chair.
Just when you're sure
You're going to scream,
You'll hear your Mom whisper,
"Now don't make a scene."

Schedules

Although I mark my calendar
For each special date,
I get there too early
Or else very late.
I try to make schedules
For each day and night.
So why don't I ever
Get it just right?

Second Shelf

I'd like to read
That book again.
It helped me
Understand myself.
I keep it here
In my tall bookcase,
On the always reachable
Second shelf.

Seems-Like Tab

Today seems like Monday.
Yesterday did, too.
Because it wasn't a holiday,
Just the day we once knew.
Holidays happen,
But who knows when?
My seems-like tab
Is stuck again.

Selective Memory

Selective memory
Reveals but a flash.
Important details
Dropped into the trash.
I kept the things
I should forget,
And lost the ones
I should have kept.

Self-Improvement

Practice your cooking
And you'll eat finer food.
Alter your attitude.
You'll improve your mood.
Think first of others.
De-emphasize "me".
Your life can become
What you want it to be.

Serendipity

I received this flower
Yesterday
Totally, entirely unexpectedly.
On your birthday today,
I'll give it to you.
Probably totally
Unexpectedly too.

Set of Eight

Last year I painted
This lovely plate.
It's the first design
In a set of eight.
I meant to finish
Every one.
But that was easier
Said than done.

Shrinkage

It's one hundred percent cotton.
Without a thought or a blink,
I got an extra-large size.
I was sure it would shrink.
Now it's inches too long,
And eons too wide.
The only thing shrinking
Is this person inside.

Siesta

I went to bed late
And woke up early.
Now it's noon
And I'm feeling surly.
No need to fret.
The worst is past.
Right after lunch
I can fall asleep fast.

Simple Faith

My faith is simple,
Childlike, and plain.
No questions to ask.
No need to explain.
I don't ask why
Things turn out as they do.
Not "Why me, Oh Lord?"
Just "Lord, keep me near You."

Sisterhood of Strength

Ladies in their eighties
Coming down the hall.
Some are strong and sturdy.
Some are frail and small.
Personalities and aptitudes
As different as can be.
But united in a sisterhood
Of strength for you and me.

Sixty-Five Year Romance

In 1940,
They met at a dance.
And there began
A sixty-five year romance.
With no regrets
And no need for dread,
Hand in hand,
They're moving ahead.

Snow

Flakes, crystals, and flurries.
It's going to snow.
Haven't seen it for years,
But I instinctively know.
Drifts, sleds, and snowmen.
Crunchy sidewalks to clear.
Just a dream or a memory.
It won't happen here.

Somewhere Beyond

Somewhere beyond
Today's trials.
Somewhere that's
Steady and flat.
Somewhere all
Things have solutions.
I'm trying to
Focus on that.

Speak Slowly

When you're talking, please speak slowly.
Do not fear you might offend.
Though I hear the words you're saying,
I need some time to comprehend.
I don't require a hearing aid,
Like so many of us do,
But I listen at a slower speed
Than I once was able to.

Squashed From the Top

Shrinking height
And increasing weight
Is not a formula
For looking great.
Address the problem!
It's very strange
To be squashed from the top.
Something must change!

Sticky Notes

Pale yellow sticky notes
Bright ones, too
Help me to know
What I should do.
They're on my mirror.
They're on my door.
I must remember
To get some more.

Stock Your Pockets

Stock your pockets
With tissues and pills,
A couple of cough drops,
Spot remover for spills.
If you have no pockets,
You would be wise
To stock your socks!
Just improvise!

Storms

The storms I have seen
In my four-score five
Make me grateful
That I am alive.
One tornado, two hurricanes,
Three fires, and a flood
Which left behind
A river of mud.

Sunday Bells

Trilling and warbling
Birds at dawn,
Tunes ringing out
From the carillon,
Chimes in a church tower
Sounding their knells,
The variegated music
Of the Sunday bells.

Sunrise

Through my window blinds
I saw the sun rise.
Pale orange streaks
Against pale blue skies.
Then behind the roofs,
A ball of fire appeared.
Treetops turned gold.
The horizon cleared.

Super-sized Stores

I don't shop at Wal-Mart
Or Sam's Club or Sears.
These super-sized stores
Arouse anxiety and fears.
How could I find things?
Would I wait on myself?
Or might a helpful employee
Lead me to the right shelf?

Table Number One

Today I thought
It would be fun
To sit at
Table Number One.
And here I am
Waiting to see
Who will come
And sit with me.

Tangled Thought

Temporarily
Twisted thinking
Turns into
Totally tangled thought.
So I may not
Know what I'm saying
Even though
You think I ought.

Tattling

I didn't intend
To be tattling.
I was just telling
Something good.
But sometimes
Innocent teasing
Can be woefully
Misunderstood.

Ten After Eight

It's ten after eight.
I don't want to be late
For the meeting
That's starting at nine.
Brush teeth and comb hair.
Decide what to wear.
The first thing that fits
Will be fine.

Texas A&M

Holsters, guns, and cowboy hats,
Fancy boots and spurs
Proclaim a young man's entry
Into the world of westerners.
A bravado that will never fade
Grows stronger through the years,
Bolstered by the backdrop
Of the Texas Aggie cheers.

Therapy

I'm writing more now,
Maybe more than I should.
Poems rough and unpolished
And not very good.
Maybe their function
Is to provide therapy
In this troubled transition
That terrifies me.

The Robin's Song

Thank you for letting me
Sleep all night long,
Then wake to the sound
Of the robin's song.
This is a day
That may be fine!
So thank you, Lord!
This day is mine!

The Sensible Few

As each day I re-enter
The world of my peers,
I try not to surrender
To advancing years.
I strive to stay steady.
For what I don't want to do
Is join the ranks of the restless
And leave the sensible few.

Thingamajig

Each of my treasures,
Small or big
Is a thingamabob
Or a thingamajig.
These nameless gadgets
Challenge my mind.
A reason to keep them
I must find.

Tiny Tear

Death came for my neighbor.
It was unexpected and quick.
I'm rejoicing for her,
She hadn't even been sick.
But the one tiny tear
That slipped from my eye
Won't be the only
Tear that I'll cry.

To Billie

Your farewell party
Will be today.
I must tell you goodbye,
But what can I say?
Words can't express
What you've been for me.
A beacon of light
In a stormy sea.

To The Cable Guy

My computer says
It is very upset.
It has lost its connection
To the Internet.
How to get this back
I don't have a clue.
So both of us
Are depending on you.

To Connie

How can we say what you've meant to us?
It's an unending, unforgettable list.
You can't even begin to imagine
How very much you'll be missed.
Have a happy, fulfilling retirement.
Remember the old recipe.
Do something you really love to do
And spread joy in the places you'll be.

To My Child

This isn't the way
I thought it would be.
You weren't meant to go
Ahead of me.
In all ages and places,
The natural plan
Is that parents die
Before their children can.

Too Hot, Too Cold

Clothing temperature
Is hard to control.
I can't get it right
To save my soul.
I'm overheated in wool
That I can't take off,
Or shivering in sheers
That aren't warm enough.

Turnover

Many employees
Have come and gone.
Some were promoted.
Some just moved on.
Once in a while
Somebody was fired.
And a fortunate few
Happily retired.

Use-By Date

Exploratory surgery
May be required,
But my use-by date
Has expired.
It doesn't take
A surgeon's knife
To improve
My quality of life.

Vigil

I wonder where
She is tonight.
She left this morning
Before daylight.
I'll watch and wait
Till the morning sun
Tells me another
Day has begun.

Weather Buff

I was not a trained forecaster,
Just a weather buff
Before Doppler and radar
And all that new stuff.
It was great fun
To predict rainy or breezy,
But second-guessing the weather
Never was easy.

Whatsis

Crannies and crevices
Of closet and shelf
Hold memory triggers
I packed up myself.
Quiet reminders
That time will fly.
Whatsis and doodads
From days gone by.

Where Is It?

It's in a stack or a pile
Or a very neat file
Or in a box
On the closet shelf.
With a little more time
And a heaven-sent sign,
I might be able
To find it myself.

Why Not Me?

There must be a better
Way to arrange!
Somebody do something!
We need a change!
Someone may come.
You could wait and see,
Or you could ask,
Why not me?

Winding Down

Multiple missions
Filled my life.
A long-time career,
A mother and wife.
Whirling and swirling
Though house and town,
Now I'm learning
The winding down.

A LITTLE LONGER

Introduction to PineCrest

It soon will be Christmas, 2002.
This holiday greeting from me is for you!
Though it's hardly the verse that you used to get,
There's a wee bit of rhyme in this old gal yet.

At PineCrest, a new kind of life I've begun.
I've called it home since 2001.
A better place would be hard to find.
Everything's here that I had in mind.

Chapel, plays, library, concerts and such,
Bank, market, pharmacy—they didn't miss much!
Add the best staff and best residents you'll ever meet.
What more could there be to make life complete?

When a medical visit or short errand we plan,
We are transported there by bus or by van.
And a much larger bus will take over the run
When our groups travel farther for sightseeing fun.

Activities especially dear to my heart
Are writing life stories and helping others to start.
Also welcoming newcomers, mixing people at meals,
Sending birthday notes, and creating "new deals."

I love my computer—hadn't thought that I would.
But its presence each morning helps make my day good.
The Lubbock A-J gives me West Texas news,
And I cheer when new e-mails pop up on my "views."

My family is growing. My children are well.
The new generations cause our numbers to swell.
I have seventeen grandchildren and nearly nine "greats."
Some live in Texas, some in faraway states.

But enough about me. Now what about you?
Have a blessed Christmas! Enjoy all that you do!
Stay as healthy and happy as you are able to be!
And have a very good year in 2003!

Celebrations

Birthdays, Quinceaneras, Bar Mitzvahs.
Weddings, baptisms, and births.
Anniversaries—from first to golden or more.
All milestones deserving of worth.

Memorial services, celebration of lives
Of relatives, neighbors, and friends.
Historic events, births of persons of fame.
Independence Days, victories, and trends.

Business developments, new VIPs,
Festivals—watermelon, strawberry, peach.
Accomplishments, promotions, awards, winning teams.
Recognition if you volunteer, lead, or teach.

Clear Instructions

We want to succeed,
To do everything right.
At home or at school,
Office desk or job site.

There is a simple favor
That we need to ask.
Give us clear instructions
When you give us a task.

Keep it plain, keep it simple.
Leave extra words out.
Say just what you mean.
Do not leave any doubt.

Speak slowly and clearly.
Calmly repeat.
Stay nearby. Answer questions.
Keep replies short and sweet.

Never lose patience.
Take time to get through.
Encourage, empower.
You learned. We can, too.

Crabs and Lobsters

Lots of sea critters
I never have seen.
To me, crabs and lobsters
Sound fearsome and mean.

Maybe they taste good.
People say that they do.
But I'll leave those seafoods
To folks like you.

It's doubtful that I
Ever will meet
A crab or a lobster
That I'll want to eat.

Dream

Growing up lonely
In a storybook house.
The long train trip to college.
A wedding and spouse.
That amazing first baby!
Many others to come!
Then grands and great-grands,
An incredible sum.
Living my memories,
Creating each scene,
All those years of my life
Seem to be but a dream.

For June—In a Nursing Home

Bloom where you're planted.
You'll think of a way
That you can help
Somebody today.

Because you're a nurturer,
A provider of cheer,
An encourager, listener,
Ready to hear,

You'll find all around you
People burdened with cares.
Your troubles will fade
As you listen to theirs.

Using your talents
Makes a difference—you'll see!
Life will be better
Than you thought it could be.

Friday Night Fandango

I love the old dances
That we used to do.
Just hearing their music
Thrills me anew.

The Polka and Schottische
And Texas Two-Step
Are all simple melodies
That require dancers with pep.

When I hear the first strains
Of the Cotton-Eyed Joe
My instinctive response
Is "Hop up! Let's go!"

The Varsouviana's
Gentle waltz strains
Say "Put your little foot right out,"
But my foot complains.

Though I've long been sidelined,
I'm happy to find
That words, moves, and music
Still bring joy to my mind.

Good Choices

Dear Lord, help me to make
Good choices today
In the things that I do
And the words that I say.

In each place I go,
In each message I send,
In each casual remark
To a neighbor or friend.

In the books that I read,
In the shows that I view,
Help me find those
That are pleasing to You.

And let me remember
My pledge, come what may,
Is to help someone else
In some way, every day.

You've shown me the path
That You want me to keep.
Help me stay on it.
It's now growing steep.

If I should stumble,
Lift me up, let me stand.
Let my actions and words
Be as You've planned.

Holiday Greetings
From Lufkin, Texas

A glance at the calendar
Reveals it's nearly December.
Although that appears an unlikely fix.
It seems like just yesterday
That our wish for the holiday
Was "Have a good year in 2006".

This greeting was created
In the now-designated
Texas Forest Country, region of fame.
Formerly Deep East Texas,
Or the Big Piney Woods.
Please call us now by our brand new name!

We have scores of attractions.
You can get the directions
From texasforestcountry.com
If you've considered retiring,
You'll see we're awe-inspiring
Select your new home right now and be done!

You'll find natural beauty,
Towering trees, friendly people.
Just what you're looking for.
You can be closer to Heaven
In two-thousand seven
Than you've ever been before!

Lessons From My Past

My ancestors found
The power of a word.
Written or spoken,
Envisioned or heard.
Their fingers and hands
Held pencils and pens.
Never hammer or chisel
Or scalpel or lens.
They developed careers
As missionaries and preachers
And, no surprise here,
Professors and teachers.
No artists, designers,
Engineers or MDs.
No architects, carpenters,
Not one of these.
No wholesalers, retailers,
No entrepreneuers.
And no CEOs
Showed up in their furs.
From this history I see,
It's quite clear now to me,
That they sat, read, and thought,
Then they stood, spoke, and taught.
Lacking manual dexterity,
And visual perceptual acuity,
They developed fine skills
In social security.
Genetics? Environment?

Opportunity? Inspiration?
Or a bit stronger influence?
Necessity? Deprivation?
It confirms that old saying,
Not at all out of reach,
That those who can, do.
And those who can't, teach.
This much I know,
And I'm sure you do, too.
Use your God-given gifts
In the way meant for you.
Then find new ways to share them
As you move through the years.
There's no better prevention
Of aches, pains, and fears.

News Test

Do you know it's a fact?
Verifiably true?
Or did someone just happen
To tell it to you?

Could it be harmful?
Or does it seem kind?
What sort of reaction
Is it likely to find?

If it won't measure up,
Must it still unfold?
Unless there's a good reason
It should not be told!

Occasion Dressing

Is is a cold day or a hot day?
Or a "have-to-do-a-lot" day?
A "nothing-that's-too-bright" day?
Or a "perfect-time-for-white" day?

A "why-did-I-get-up?" day?
Or "hot-coffee-in-my-cup" day?
A "quick-dressing-is-a-snap" day?
Or a "no-time-for-a-nap" day?

An "umbrella-and-a-hat" day?
Or an "anything-but-that" day?
A "my-hair-is-a-mess" day?
Or a "must-wear-the-little-black-dress" day?

It's just a "I'm-a-bit-confused" day.
Maybe Monday, maybe Tuesday.

Pickup Comin' Down The Road

She untied her apron, threw it in the corner.
Wondering if her pounding heartbeat really showed.
When she heard her Daddy shouting through the screen door,
"Think I hear his pickup comin' down the road."

In her own small kitchen where she ruled as Mother,
Children played beside her rocker as she sewed.
Crying, "Mama, can we go to meet our Daddy?
We can hear his pickup comin' down the road."

How they've passed, the golden minutes of her lifetime.
The rolling hours, the rushing days, the gathering years.
Life has given her full measure of its richness.
Joy and laughter, pain and sorrow, smiles and tears.

Now she sits alone beside a misty window.
Knowing soon she will lay down her heavy load,
And ride off with him to join those gone before them,
When she hears his pickup comin' down the road.

And together they will ride that golden highway
When she hears his pickup comin' down the road.

Playing Santa

I tried once again
To play Santa last year.
I found "just perfect" gifts
And wrapped them right here!

It didn't go well.
How I longed to escape
Tangled ribbons and tissues,
Boxes, labels, and tape.

So it's back to the catalog.
"Bill to, Ship to" for me.
Or a one-size-fits-all
Holly wreath, QVC.

The Party Crashers
(A Nonsense Rhyme)

Five dogs and ten cats
And fifty very small gnats
All went to the party with me.
We barked and we meowed,
And we buzzed 'round the crowd,
Who regarded us dubiously.

When barometers showed
Folks' annoyance o'erflowed,
Reinforcements arrived to prevail.
Dogcatchers, cat trappers, exterminators galore
Joined ten truant officers
Already hot on our trail.

We agreed to be cool,
And not play the fool,
Though we'd intended to stay there and eat.,
Snatching slivers and snacks,
Sips, straws, and small sacks,
We gracefully made our retreat.

Rat-Speak

Said Pa Rat to Ma,
"Good morning!
I hope you're feeling well,
My dear!
What can we do
To have some fun
Without causing too much fear?"

Said Ma Rat to Pa,
"I'll tell you how.
Let's just wake up
Ellen now.
It seems to me
That otherwise
She just might sleep
Through exercise!"

Added Ma Rat to Pa Rat
"You know, it never fails
You make a lot of racket
When you forget to trim your nails!"

Silly Song

Rule #36: Every night before bed, think of one thing you're grateful for that you've never been grateful for before.

For what have I not been grateful before?
Something I felt, but chose to ignore?
Something I lost, and could not restore?
Something that seemed an impossible chore?

More is less, and less is more.
That's a saying I've heard somewhere before.
But what should I now feel grateful for
That I've not been grateful for before?

There's a vacant shelf by my pantry door.
Tomorrow I go to the grocery store.
But now, that plan I can ignore,
For more is less and less is more!

This silly song makes my spirits soar.
Now I can laugh and laugh some more!
There's no "what if" and no "either/or"
When more is less and less is more!

To Bonnie Bess At 100

July 23, 2007

Our daily role model,
Upright and steady.
Faithful neighbor and friend,
Dependable, ready.
Teacher to many,
Inspiration to more.
Independence personified
On trips to the store.
Determination to walk.
No scooter needed.
The things you attempted
Nearly always succeeded!
You're a living miracle
Of our century!
We salute you and your life
Each July twenty-three!

.

To Lavern

To the lovely and charming
Lady Lavern,
My very dear
Down-the-hall neighbor,
(Whom I see every Sunday,
Right after lunch,
Chapel-bound
On the freight elevator).

All birthdays are fun,
But each most-observed one
Is a milestone
Ending in zero.

You're celebrating today
A special birthday!
You've arrived!
Have a Happy Big 8-0!

Your Gift

What happy activity
Do you love to do?
Could it bring joy
To someone else too?
You have been given
A gift of the heart.
A skill, an ability,
A knowledge, an art.

What game do you play?
What craft can you do?
What brings a special
Satisfaction to you?
Are you a good visitor?
Do you listen and care?
There could be a real
Opportunity there.

Can you talk about books?
Maybe old, maybe new?
Somebody's looking
For someone like you.
If you can succeed
In finding the way,
You'll receive a true blessing
Every day.

978-0-595-46123-3
0-595-46123-9

Printed in the United States
102296LV00003B/217-234/A